JEAN LAFFITE
THE PIRATE WHO SAVED AMERICA

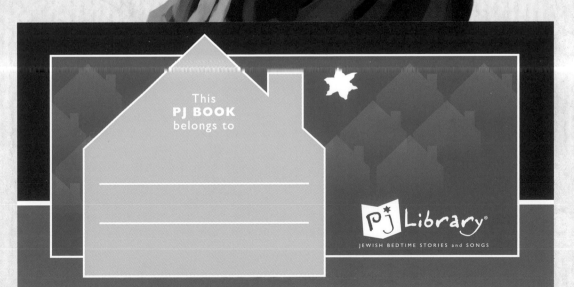

By SUSAN GOLDMAN RUBIN
Illustrated by JEFF HIMMELMAN

Abrams Books for Young Readers · New York

A great number of Jewish people became pirates of the Caribbean. They had been kicked out of Spain, then other parts of Europe, and many had no homeland. For this reason, they detested Spain and gladly hired themselves out as privateers to seize and rob Spanish ships. One of the Jewish pirates was even a rabbi who brought a Jewish chef along to prepare kosher meals and, on land, held services in his house. Another, years later, was Jean Laffite.

As a little boy, Jean, born in the early 1780s and the youngest of eight children, dreamed of being a pirate. So did his brother, Pierre. They admired their oldest brother, Alexander, a pirate of the Caribbean. When Alexander came home to Port-au-Prince, he told Jean and Pierre incredible tales about his voyages.

"He always brought us gifts," said Jean. Alexander probably brought the boys a parrot, or a parakeet, or even a monkey as a souvenir from his travels.

Even though pirating was a common business in those days, their Grandma Zora strongly disapproved. She raised Jean and his older brothers and sisters after the death of their mother. Grandma Zora told stories, too. Hers were about the family's suffering in Spain and how they had to practice their Jewish faith in secret. Like many others, they had fled to the New World and had settled in Port-au-Prince in Saint-Domingue (later renamed Haiti).

Because of Grandma Zora's stories, Jean and Pierre hated Spain. "We decided that when we grew up we would capture all vessels flying the Spanish flag," said Jean.

Grandma Zora, however, wanted the boys to be well educated and use writing to help others. She sent them to good schools. So Alexander had to secretly teach the boys about pirating.

By the time Jean was sixteen and Pierre was eighteen, they had begun taking voyages with Alexander and had sailed to New Orleans. "I missed Grandmother a great deal," said Jean, "and she wept everytime I went aboard a ship."

Alexander was a type of pirate called a privateer. He had a letter of marque, or license, from France giving him permission to capture Spanish ships. In return, he agreed to share the loot with the French government. Flying the French flag, Jean and his brothers set sail to find Spanish merchant vessels and warships.

"The first vessel we captured was owned by a Spanish family of Saint-Domingue," said Jean. Armed with pistols tucked in their belts, knives up their sleeves, and cutlasses strapped to their wrists, they jumped on board the schooner. Alexander demanded to know where the cargo was hidden. He fired his pistol. The terrified captain finally surrendered his stash of gold, coffee, and cinnamon.

Sometimes Jean and Pierre signed on as sailors with other privateers so that they could "learn the trade." Unlike most pirates, Jean was as polite and gentlemanly aboard ship as he was in port. On a voyage to St. Croix, Jean met a Danish Jewish girl, Christina Levine. They fell in love, married, and within a year had a son. Pierre was now married, too, and the families lived comfortably in Port-au-Prince.

In April 1801, Jean and Pierre took command of a ship jointly. Their uncle Reyne was captain of another vessel, and together the ships sailed west flying the French flag.

After two weeks at sea, Jean and his brother and uncle spotted a Spanish sloop of war on the horizon. They raised their sails. "With a good wind behind us we were able to keep up a high speed," said Jean. As they drew closer, Jean fired a cannon, a warning signal for the warship to heave to. Uncle Reyne gave orders through a "speaking tube" for the Spanish officers to surrender. The frightened crew of the Spanish ship ran around in all directions. Men scurried belowdecks to hide. Others jumped overboard.

Jean and Pierre threw their lines over the railing of the Spanish warship. Grappling hooks caught the rigging. "Prepare to board!" ordered Uncle Reyne.

They forced the captain to show them where the treasure was hidden. Jean and Pierre found gold, silver, and bronze, as well as "boxes filled with gold doubloons [Spanish coins]." Best of all, they discovered "secret sailing papers" that contained information to help them capture more Spanish vessels. With the sloop of war in tow, they sailed toward home.

As soon as they arrived in Port-au-Prince, Jean hugged and kissed his wife and grandmother.

He always carried with him the Hebrew Bible that Grandma Zora had given him. On the flyleaf he wrote, "I owe all my ingenuity to the great intuition of my Jewish Spanish grandmother." He never forgot his grandma's ideals.

Over the next few years, Jean and Pierre captured many ships and earned a fortune. At the age of twenty-two, Jean fought his first duel. With his sword drawn, he boarded a Spanish ship. The ship pitched and rolled as Jean and the officer clanked swords. Jean won the duel without killing the officer. He took all the sailors prisoner, and they became members of his crew.

In 1804, Grandma Zora died. Jean and his family mourned her greatly. Jean decided it was time for a change, so he planned to move to France with his wife, sons, and newborn daughter. He bought a ship, loaded her with everything he owned, and sailed off with his family.

After one week at sea, a Spanish man-of-war chased them and attacked. "The Spaniards captured us," said Jean. "They took everything . . . even my wife's jewels." Then they put Jean and his wife and children on a low, sandy island and left them there to starve. They were marooned! Stranded! A pirate's worst fear. Jean was sure they would die.

Luckily, a few days later, an American schooner sailed by and rescued them. From then on, Jean felt great loyalty to America.

The ship took them to New Orleans. Jean's wife had become very sick with fever during the ordeal, and she died three weeks after they arrived in the city. Jean vowed revenge against the Spanish ship and its crew for what they had done to him, his family, and especially his wife.

To Jean's surprise, the whole Laffite family had come to New Orleans. Jean's sister and sister-in-law took care of his children.

Pierre had lost his ship, too—Governor William Claiborne had accused him of smuggling (which was true) and had taken his brig. Pierre had sneaked stolen goods into New Orleans without paying the government a tax. Now that the United States owned Louisiana, Governor Claiborne was in charge. He despised pirates and wanted to rid New Orleans of them.

To support themselves, Jean and Pierre got jobs with the United States Customs Service and even arrested other smugglers!

By 1806, the brothers had enough money to buy a schooner, and they went back into business as privateers. More than ever, Jean burned with the desire to capture Spanish vessels, especially the warship that had contributed to his wife's death. "So long as I live I am at war with Spain," he said.

Jean, Pierre, and their crew sailed to the city-state of Cartagena in Colombia to get a letter of marque. Colombia had been ruled by Spain and was struggling to become independent. So the government welcomed the help of privateers like Jean. Flying the Colombian flag, he set out in his brig, *Misère* (Misery), to seize his prey. Soon he caught a Spanish schooner. He renamed her *Dorade*, the "Golden Dolphin Fish." *Dorade* became his favorite ship.

As Jean and his brothers swept across the Gulf of Mexico in their ships, they took one Spanish schooner after another. At last, in 1807, Jean hunted down the hated man-of-war. After a fierce battle, Jean forced the Spanish captain to surrender. He had finally avenged his wife's death.

Within three years, Jean and Pierre, working as a team, had plundered dozens of Spanish ships. Their older brothers Alexander and René joined their fleet.

Jean became a favorite citizen in New Orleans. He opened a blacksmith shop in town and became acquainted with people in the community. With his stylish clothes, polished nails, and charming manners, he won respect and was well liked. At his grand home above the blacksmith shop and at Maison Rouge, his mansion in Barataria Bay, he gave dinner parties that were attended by leading citizens.

At that time, Spanish ships carried African slaves as cargo. Although outlawed in many places, slavery was an accepted practice in the southern United States and the Caribbean islands. Jean remembered his grandma's teaching and said, "I have never approved of the idea of trading and holding slaves." Yet as a privateer who seized Spanish ships that held slaves along with the goods he actually sought, he wound up selling slaves to southerners.

In 1807, a law was passed making it illegal to bring new slaves into the United States. However, New Orleans plantation owners and rich businessmen still wanted them. So on certain days of the week they secretly went to the Laffites' pirate hideaway in Barataria Bay to buy slaves. They also bought smuggled goods, such as furniture, fancy clothes, and jewelry.

Barataria Bay was a perfect pirate hideout. The islands Grand Terre and Grand Isle formed natural barriers to the bay. The surrounding marshes were filled with alligators and poisonous snakes. Only Jean and his privateers knew how to slip through the twisting, shallow bayous in their pirogues, which are flat-bottom boats. They transferred booty from the big ships they had raided into pirogues and rowboats and then stashed the loot in warehouses on Grand Terre.

Around this time, between five hundred and a thousand buccaneers were hiding out in Barataria Bay. Some of them had been there for years. Others were new arrivals from France and Italy or former slaves who had become pirates. Whereas Jean wore the clothes of a gentleman, most pirates wore gold earrings, striped shirts, and colorful bandannas tied around their heads. They fought constantly and stole from each other. Many could not read or write and signed their name with an X. Jean, with his calm manner and wisdom, was often called upon to settle quarrels.

Around 1808, on a hillside in Barataria, the first pirate convention was held, and the sea robbers, including Jean's brothers and uncles, chose Jean as their leader. Everyone called him *"Bos"* (Boss) and followed his orders. He could speak four languages—English, French, Spanish, and Italian—which helped him control the cutthroat ruffians.

The Baratarians, as they called themselves, did more business than any merchant in Louisiana but paid no taxes to the state or to the United States government. Governor Claiborne was furious that they were breaking the law, and he offered a reward of $500 for the capture of Jean Laffite. With his good sense of humor, Jean responded by promising a reward of $5,000 for the capture of Governor Claiborne. Nothing came of it.

Finally, Governor Claiborne appealed to the newly elected president, James Madison, to rid the country of these pirates.

The United States, however, had become involved in the War of 1812 and had bigger problems. The war started because Britain was fighting with France, and, among other things, the British forced American sailors to join their navy. The British also tried to turn Americans against President Madison. Most of all, they wanted to reclaim American land as part of the United Kingdom.

In the summer of 1814, British warships and thousands of well-trained, experienced British troops arrived on the East Coast. British soldiers, called redcoats, marched on the nation's capital and burned down the White House, the Capitol, and the Library of Congress. Next, they attacked Baltimore. They also wanted to capture New Orleans, so they could control the Mississippi River and the entire West.

At first, people in Louisiana didn't believe it would happen. But Jean did. From his perch on top of Grande Terre Island, he spotted British warships off the coast of Louisiana. Quickly, he sent a message to Washington, D.C., with the information. His messenger never came back. Jean tried again. "My warning messages were either ignored, or more probably they never reached the officers," he said.

On September 3, 1814, at around ten o'clock in the morning, an armed British brig with two officers aboard sailed into Barataria Bay. The British realized that only Jean and his buccaneers knew how to navigate the twisting bayous and canals leading to New Orleans. Waving a white flag of truce, the commander and his interpreter came ashore. Jean's men angrily shouted to take the officers prisoner. Jean, however, respected their flag of truce, and took the officers to his dwelling. They offered Jean a rank of captain in the British Royal Navy, a gift of thirty thousand dollars (more than two million dollars today!), and a full pardon for him and his Baratarians for their

crime of piracy if they would help beat the Americans. Jean pretended to consider the offer. Meanwhile, he rushed a letter to Governor Claiborne telling him of the proposal and also that the British were planning to invade New Orleans. The governor didn't believe him.

Jean sent another letter to Governor Claiborne offering his services and those of his buccaneers. Again, the governor ignored him. Then Jean received news from a pirate spy in Havana, Cuba. The letter said that the British were planning to enlist thousands of native peoples and slaves in Florida to attack the cities of Pensacola, Mobile, and New Orleans. "You have not a moment to lose," wrote the spy.

Jean hurried this letter to Governor Claiborne, who at last believed him. General Andrew Jackson was sent to protect New Orleans. Jackson, known as Old Hickory because he was said to be as tough as that kind of wood, led his ragtag army of volunteers to New Orleans. When Jean's lawyer asked Jackson to let Jean and the Baratarians fight with his backwoodsmen, Jackson said he wanted nothing to do with the "banditti." However, even Governor Claiborne urged him to accept Jean's offer to "march against the enemy."

Finally, Jackson invited Jean to meet with him at his headquarters. Jean said that he and all the Baratarians were ready "to defend the country and its inhabitants." And, according to a witness, "the General accepted their offers."

Jean shared his knowledge of the bayous and swamplands with Jackson. He prepared maps and showed the general where to build levees and barricades. Jean also supplied him with cannons, gunpowder, and his best sailors and artillerymen.

On January 8, 1815, just before dawn, the Battle of New Orleans began. The three thousand uniformed British troops greatly outnumbered the scruffy American army, which was made up of backwoodsmen, pirates, freed slaves, gunboat sailors, and a few women from New Orleans. British drums rattled as Jackson's army and the Baratarians crouched along the levee in groups of four. Dense fog kept them concealed. The British fired a rocket to signal the attack. Cannon fire filled the air. Guns boomed. Musket balls whizzed by.

Within a half an hour, the battle was over. The Americans had won! They had killed 2,500 British soldiers, but only thirteen Americans had died. The remaining British redcoats ran away, claiming they were following an order to retreat.

General Jackson thanked Jean and his buccaneers for their effort. "[The Baratarians] have performed their duty with zeal and bravery," he said. By January 18, the last of the British soldiers had left Louisiana, and the war ended soon after. America had reestablished its independence.

On January 23, all of New Orleans celebrated. Jean and the Baratarians marched in a parade along with Jackson's soldiers. Bands played "Yankee Doodle," and ladies showered the men with camellia petals. That evening there was a Victory Ball and Jean danced until two o'clock in the morning.

In February, President Madison received Jackson's account of the battle, and he fully pardoned Jean and all the Baratarians who had fought and granted them citizenship. In his proclamation, President Madison praised the pirates' "traits of courage and fidelity" and "good and loyal service to the country."

From then on, Jean Laffite was known as the Hero of New Orleans, a pirate turned patriot.

Grandma Zora would have been proud.

AUTHOR'S NOTE

Resource material is scant on details of Jean Laffite's day-to-day life, so I used other sources about pirating at that time—how ships were attacked and boarded, and what clothing pirates wore. I did find articles and books about Jean by noted scholars (one of them a rabbi!) and a recent publication on the history of Jewish pirates of the Caribbean that gave me a broader view. I also read about Sephardim, as Jews originally from Spain and neighboring countries are called. In the fifteenth century, they were forced to convert to Catholicism, but they secretly practiced Judaism. These were Jean's ancestors. Spaniards gave them the insulting name *Marranos* (pigs). And this is why Jean hated and targeted the Spanish ships.

After saving New Orleans, Jean and his buccaneers moved to Galveston Island, Texas, in 1817 and set up a new pirate kingdom. One of Jean's captains mistakenly attacked a Mexican ship carrying cargo that belonged to American merchants. So the American government ordered Jean and his men to leave Galveston. It is said that before Jean sailed away he threw gold bars and jewels into the sea, and buried more treasure on the beach. To this day, people still search for Jean's loot.

Some historians claim that Jean died in the late 1820s. Others say that he spread the rumor himself so that he could lead a peaceful life in disguise. It is believed that Jean and Pierre traveled for a while, then settled in Saint Louis, Missouri, and that Jean gave up privateering and went into the business of manufacturing and selling gunpowder. He changed his name to John Lafflin so that people would not recognize him. According to this school of thought, on June 7, 1832, he married his second wife, Emma Mortimore, a young non-Jewish woman he had known for years, and they had three sons.

Little is known about Jean's religious life as a Jew in his adult years. We do know from records that John and Emma Lafflin belonged to an antislavery association. The paradox of Jean's attitude toward slavery has never been explained adequately. Louisiana poet and scholar Rodger Kamenetz calls it "an uncomfortable point." During Jean's years of privateering, he captured slaves from Spanish ships and sold them. "In ugly truth," writes Kamenetz, "he was a slave smuggler." Yet from Jean's point of view, he was releasing slaves from the cruelty of the Spaniards. He wrote, "I sold the slaves that were taken by our boats, for almost nothing . . . I do not believe in profiting from human bondage." This contradiction has never been fully made clear, and, of course, we can't soft-pedal this part of his story.

In later life, Jean became a labor leader, active in the International Working Men's Association. He wanted to be remembered for the good that he had done.

From 1845 to 1850, he wrote a journal in French for his grandchildren to give them "a true account" of his adventures as a pirate "with the understanding that they would not release it until one hundred and seven years" had passed. Finally, Jean had fulfilled his grandma's wish for him to be a writer.

According to a note inscribed on the flyleaf of the family Christian Bible, Jean died on May 5, 1854. In 1958, a great-grandson of Jean's named John A. Lafflin inherited the journal. He had it translated into English and published. The original manuscript is on display at the Sam Houston Regional Library and Research Center at Liberty, Texas. This book is based largely on that journal, Jean Laffite's own story of a Jewish pirate and patriot.

BIBLIOGRAPHY

Books

denotes material of interest to younger readers

Arthur, Stanley Clisby. *Jean Laffite, Gentleman Rover*. New Orleans: Harmanson, 1952.

* Butterfield, Moira. *Pirates & Smugglers*. Boston: Kingfisher, 2005.

* Clifford, Barry, and Kenneth J. Kinkor with Sharon Simpson. *Real Pirates*. Washington, D.C.: National Geographic, 2007.

Cordingly, David. *Under the Black Flag: The Romance and the Reality of Life Among the Pirates*. New York: Random House, 2006.

Davis, William C. *The Pirates Laffite*. New York: Harcourt, 2005.

Gosse, Philip. *The History of Piracy*. Mineola, New York: Dover, 2007.

Groom, Winston. *Patriotic Fire: Andrew Jackson and Jean Laffite at the Battle of New Orleans*. New York: Knopf, 2006.

Korn, Bertram Wallace. *The Early Jews of New Orleans*. Waltham, Mass.: American Jewish Historical Society, 1969.

Kritzler, Edward. *Jewish Pirates of the Caribbean*. New York: Doubleday, 2008.

Laffite, Jean. *The Journal of Jean Laffite*. Oakdale, La.: Dog Wood Press, 1994; originally published as a facsimile by Vantage Press, 1958.

Lewis, Jon E., ed. *The Mammoth Book of Pirates*. New York: Carroll & Graf, 2006.

* Pickering, David. *Pirates*. London: HarperCollins, 2006.

Prinz, Joachim. *The Secret Jews*. New York: Random House, 1973.

* Ross, Nola Mae Wittler. *Jean Laffite: Louisiana Buccaneer*. Lake Charles, La.: self-published, 1990.

Sharfman, I. Harold. *Jews on the Frontier*. Chicago: Henry Regnery, 1977.

* Weintraub, Aileen. *Jean Lafitte: Pirate-Hero of the War of 1812*. New York: PowerKids Press, 2002.

Articles

Geringer, Joseph. "Pirate and Patriot." In *Jean Laffite: Gentleman Pirate of New Orleans*. Gangsters & Outlaws/Cops and Other Characters, 2007 Courtroom Television Network LLC.

Glick, Edward Bernard. "The Jewish Pirate." Republished in *SA-SIG Newsletter* (January 2010): 10–11. www.bnaiabraham.net/whatsnew/jean%20lafitte.htm.

Kamenetz, Rodger. "A Jewish Pirate." *Louisiana Literature*, vol. 10, no. 2 (1993): 21–24.

Wills, Adam. "Ahoy, Mateys! Thar Be Jewish Pirates!" JewishJournal.com, Sept. 14, 2006.

PLACES TO VISIT TO FIND OUT MORE ABOUT
JEAN LAFFITE

❖❀✠❀❖

Chalmette Battlefield, site of the Battle of New Orleans, and Chalmette National Cemetery, 8606 West St. Bernard Highway, Chalmette, La.

Grand Terre Island, Grand Isle State Park, La.

Jean Lafitte National Historical Park and Preserve, Barataria Preserve, 6588 Barataria Boulevard, Marrero, La.

Lafitte's Blacksmith Shop, 941 Bourbon Street, New Orleans.

Sam Houston Regional Library and Research Center, Liberty, Tex.

INDEX

❖❀✠❀❖

For Buddy Gilson
—S. G. R.

For Dad. Your dedication to your craft has been an inspiration all my life.
—J. H.

❦❧☠❦❧

About the Illustrations

My painting process takes place almost entirely in Photoshop, using a pen tool called a Wacom Tablet. I start by creating rough sketches from my imagination. Once the publisher approves the sketches, I hire a few models to pose for reference, and I scour the Internet for photos of the locations I'll be painting as well as examples of the clothing, hairstyles, etc., of the period. Once all my references are in place, I revise my original sketches and throw down large swaths of color. The areas I want the viewer to focus on I'll tighten up, but the backgrounds can stay loose and painterly.

❦❧☠❦❧

Library of Congress Cataloging-in-Publication Data
Rubin, Susan Goldman.
Jean Lafitte : the pirate who saved America / by Susan Goldman Rubin ;
illustrated by Jeff Himmelman.
p. cm.
Includes bibliographical references and index.
ISBN 978-0-8109-9733-2 (alk. paper)
1. Lafitte, Jean—Juvenile literature. 2. Pirates—Louisiana—Biography—Juvenile literature. 3. Pirates—Texas—Biography—Juvenile literature. 4. New Orleans, Battle of, New Orleans, La., 1815—Juvenile literature.
5. Privateering—Mexico, Gulf of—History—19th century—Juvenile literature. I. Howell, Troy, ill. II. Title.
F374.L2.R83 2011
976.3'05092—dc22
[B]
2010037693

ISBN for the 2018 PJ Library paperback edition: 978-1-4197-1421-4

Text copyright © 2012 Susan Goldman Rubin
Illustrations copyright © 2012 Jeff Himmelman
Book design by Maria T. Middleton

Printed and bound in China
10 9 8 7 6 5 4 3 2

ABRAMS The Art of Books
195 Broadway, New York, NY 10007
abramsbooks.com

071827.2K2/B526/A8